Good Guide Dogs

by Caleb Graham

HOUGHTON MIFFLIN HARCOURT
School Publishers

PHOTOGRAPHY CREDITS: Cover © Jim Craigmyle/Corbis 1 Altrendo Images/Getty Images. 2 © Photodisc/SuperStock. 3 ©John Nordell/The Image Works. 5 © Jim Craigmyle/Corbis. 6 © Paul Souders/Corbis. 7 Tracy Morgan © Dorling Kindersley. 8 Getty Images. 9 DAVID GRAY/Reuters /Landov. 10 ©PA/Topham/The Image Works. 11 Altrendo Images/ Getty Images. 13 Marmaduke St. John/Alamy. 14 © Jim Craigmyle/Corbis. (bkgd) © Photodisc/SuperStock.

Printed in China

ISBN-10: 0-547-25374-5
ISBN-13: 978-0-547-25374-9

13 14 15 16 0940 18 17 16 15 14 13
4500443494

Dog owners love their pets for many reasons. Dogs can be good friends to people and fun to play with. Lots of dogs can perform tricks.

But some dogs do things that are very special. Some dogs spend their lives helping people.

Dogs Helping People

Having a disability means that a person is not able to do something such as seeing or hearing. These people may need assistance, or help, doing tasks like finding their way down crowded sidewalks or hearing a doorbell ring.

A dog trained to help a person with a disability is called an *assistance dog*. These dogs help people who are disabled perform tasks that they might not be able to do easily on their own.

An assistance dog helps guide a man who cannot see.

Guide Dogs

The best-known type of assistance dog is a *guide dog*, also called a *seeing-eye dog*. A guide dog assists someone who cannot see. The dog acts like the person's eyes, guiding the person while he or she walks. If there is another person or an object in the person's way, the dog will gently guide the person safely around the obstacle.

Laws for Guide Dogs

In many places in the United States, dogs are not allowed in restaurants or on public transportation such as buses. But because guide dogs are so important to their partners—the people they are helping—there are special laws for these dogs. These laws allow the dogs to go into restaurants with their partners and to ride on buses and trains.

A guide dog is lying quietly next to its partner in a restaurant.

Dogs have always been social animals.

Humans realized long ago that dogs had certain qualities that were helpful to people. Dogs can see and hear better than humans. Dogs have the ability to find things by smelling them. These natural qualities helped dogs survive in the wild. And, in general, dogs are very social animals. That means they like to be around other dogs and people.

Some breeds, or types, of dogs are better as guide dogs than other breeds. Guide dogs usually have to be large in order to guide their owners through crowds. They need to be strong and obedient, or able to follow commands.

German shepherds and Labrador retrievers are two of the breeds used most often as guide dogs. These dogs are strong, attentive, and loyal. These qualities make them great teammates for a person with a disability.

A Labrador retriever, on the left, meets a German shepherd.

How a Guide Dog is Trained

Most guide dogs are raised from puppies to do their jobs. When a dog is about a year old, it begins its training.

First, trainers work with a dog to teach it the tasks it will need to know in order to help a person with a disability. The dog will learn to stop at street corners and to walk around obstacles such as ladders and bushes. During training, a dog may whine and his legs may start to quiver. The dog has to practice over and over.

Puppies being trained as guide dogs learn to follow human partners.

Guide dogs are taught not to be distracted by other dogs or people.

Early on, a guide dog has to learn not to misbehave. A guide dog can't get excited about distractions in its environment such as loud noises or interesting smells. The dog has to stay calm in all situations. A guide dog cannot snap at people when it is upset or frightened.

A guide dog practices guiding its human partner through an obstacle course.

Next, each dog meets a possible partner. The partner and dog will spend time training together. Often, partners will come to stay at the guide-dog training center.

The dog and the person get to know each other and learn to trust each other. Together, they become a team. A trainer comes along on trips to supervise the partners and make suggestions. The new partners start to get attached to each other as they learn.

Oddly enough, one of the most important things a guide dog must learn to do is disobey. It sounds strange, but it's true!

This skill is called *intelligent disobedience*. A guide dog might need to disobey in order to save its partner's life. For example, if a partner tells the dog to go ahead and cross a busy street but the dog knows that it is unsafe, the dog has to refuse to obey.

A guide dog needs to know how to keep its partner safe near busy streets.

Finally, when the training period is complete, the dog goes to its new home with its partner. The dog has to get used to a new home environment. This often includes new people such as the friends and family of the dog's new partner. It can take a few months until the dog feels confident and comfortable. But soon the dog and partner will form a strong, lasting relationship.

More Dogs That Help

Guide dogs aren't the only kind of assistance dogs. Some assistance dogs help people who are sick by making them feel better. These dogs are called *therapy dogs*. Therapy dogs visit nursing homes and hospitals. Other dogs work with police officers. They patrol the streets together. At the end of a 12-hour work shift, the dogs are ready for a rest!

Two therapy dogs cheer up a boy in the hospital.

Freedom and Independence

People with disabilities are like everyone else. They just have to learn to do some things a little differently. That's where assistance dogs, such as guide dogs, can help. These loyal, determined animals allow their partners to move through the world with the freedom and independence that everyone deserves.

Responding

TARGET SKILL Author's Purpose

What was the author's purpose in writing this book? Copy the chart below. Write another detail from the book about things a guide dog does.

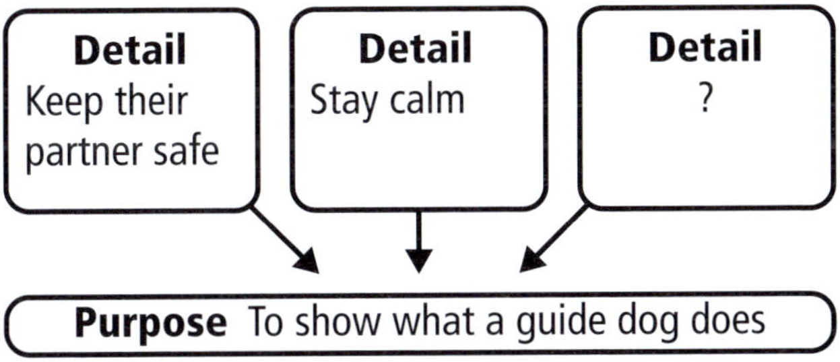

Write About It

Text to World Think of jobs that school children can do to help each other or other people. Write a paragraph describing one of those jobs.

TARGET VOCABULARY

ability	patrol
loyal	quiver
lying	shift
partners	snap

TARGET SKILL **Author's Purpose** Use text details to tell why an author writes a book.

TARGET STRATEGY **Summarize** Tell the important parts of the text in your own words.

GENRE **Informational text** gives factual information about a topic.